GROWING UP FOR GROWN-UPS
(extra) Ordinary People Who Had
The Courage To Create A Life They Love

By Mimi Rossi

Growing Up For Grown Ups
(extra) Ordinary People Who Had The Courage
To Create A Life They Love
Copyright © 2015, 2016 by Michelle Rossi

All rights reserved. Except as permitted under U.S. Copyright Act of 1976, no part of this publication may be reproduced, distributed, or transmitted in any form or by any means, or stored in a database or retrieval system, without the prior written permission of the publisher.

Limit of Liability/Disclaimer of Warranty: While the publisher and author have used their best efforts in preparing this book, they make no representations or warranties with respect to the accuracy or completeness of the contents of this book and specifically disclaim any implied warranties or merchantability or fitness for a particular purpose. No warranty may be created or extended by sales representatives or written sales materials. The advice and strategies contained herein may not be suitable for your situation. You should consult with a professional where appropriate. Neither the publisher nor author shall be liable for any loss or profit or any other commercial damages, including but not limited to special, incidental, consequential, or other damages.

For general information on our other products and services please contact us:

Phone: 1-800-394-5709
E-mail: info@growingupforgrownups.com
Web: www.growingupforgrownups.com

Book Design by Joseph Reidhead & Company Publishers and Michelle Rossi
Illustrations by Michelle Rossi
Editing by Jessica Pilla
Revised: June 2016
ISBN: 978-0-9891420-1-4
Printed in the United States of America

DEDICATION

This book is dedicated to all those who are on the cusp of living the life they love. Remember, the only limitations you have are the ones you place on yourself. You *can* do it!

CONTENTS

Dedication v
Foreword ix
Preface xiii
Acknowledgements xv
1 The Big Picture 1
2 Business Owner, Real Estate Broker, Investor, Philanthropist 5
3 Dream Teacher, Coach, Author 11
4 Paralegal, Licensed Notary, Dabbling Artist 19
5 Mother, Wife, Small Business Owner, Voice Over Artist 25
6 Assistant District Attorney 31
7 Librarian, Husband, Father 37
8 Attorney, Social Worker 43
9 Creative Entrepreneur 49
10 Police Officer, Husband, Father 57
11 Law Professional, Wife, Mother 63
12 Systems Developer/IT, Professional Poker Player, DJ/Producer 71
13 Artist, Writer, Entrepreneur 79
14 What's your story? 85
15 Reflection 91

FOREWORD

When Mimi Rossi approached me about writing the Foreword for her book, Growing Up for Grown-Ups: (extra) Ordinary People Who Had the Courage to Create a Life They Love, I was humbled. Mimi has a truly extraordinary ability to draw people to her, all the while gently challenging them to take life to the next level.

This book is a precious collection of short, autobiographical essays written by a diverse group of people who refused to give up their dream of a rewarding and fulfilling life. Author Mimi Rossi gathered these touching, reassuring, and impressive real-life stories together in order to inspire and galvanize us to take action in our own lives.

Whether you dream of starting your own business, yearn for a career path change, or feel driven by a burning desire to pursue the arts, this book contains poignant examples from individuals with occupations everyone can relate to: librarian, paralegal, real estate investor, police officer, and teacher. Yet, these same individuals could also be called innovators, change-agents, progressives and creative thinkers because they did not give up on their dreams.

If you're someone who is inspired by the lives of others, this book is a must read. At the end of every chapter, Mimi shares her own succinct insights and straightforward, relevant advice that we can use to move our own lives forward. If you are looking for change but don't know where to start, it is chock full of hope and encouragement, plus in Chapter 10, Mimi puts the icing on the cake by providing a step-by-step example to get you started.

As a life and business coach, I often share this quote by

Howard Thurman: "Don't ask yourself what the world needs. Ask yourself what makes you come alive, and then go do that. Because what the world needs are people who have come alive."

The incredible life stories assembled in this book will inspire you to passionately shout "yes!" to that little voice inside you that wants more. Then Mimi will motivate you to get out there and create a life to love!

Eileen Boyle
*Life & Business Coach, Business Consultant,
Social Media & Online Marketing Strategist, and Author*

About Eileen

Midlife & Menopause Coach Eileen Boyle uses her personal experiences as a roadmap for helping 40 to 65 year old women successfully navigate life's often tricky and stressful path. Whether you're facing a single personal crisis, health problem or business challenge, or you're juggling multiple issues simultaneously; she will draw on her extensive expertise in order to help you create a life you will truly love!

Learn more: www.MidlifeandMenopauseCoach.com

PREFACE

In almost every species, both the male and the female have their own specific roles. Human beings are no different. As we evolved, it became the man's role to hunt and gather and the woman's role to take care of the family and home. Over time, we have settled into these roles and they became natural for us. They didn't think about what they liked or didn't like - it became instinct, natural for the man to hunt and gather and the woman to take care of the family and create a home. And then there was that rogue person that thought differently, had the burning desire to do something different and deviate from that role. Instead of letting that desire die inside them - as possibly others before had done - they did something about it. They chose to step out of the norm, out of their comfort zone, and go for it. Sometimes that meant being shunned and cast out for doing or thinking differently.

Fast forward to today, we now have a society where the average person starts out in a certain field or job and sticks with it. They stick with it because, even though they get no enjoyment from it, they get complacent. The job they have is may be what they went to school for, what their parents expected of them, or what they were trained to do. They feel they don't know how to do anything else, or simply can't do anything else, so they stay stuck in that position. In the end, they lead an unhappy and unfulfilling life.

When you look at inspirational people like Bill & Melinda Gates, Oprah Winfrey, Richard Branson, Danny Thomas, or even Mother Teresa, their achievements can seem larger than life. We tend to forget that they are all ordinary human beings that just happened to do extra-ordinary things. This is why I decided to compile this book of everyday people who had the courage to change their career path and, in the long-run, their lives and the lives of others.

I truly believe that if a person is happy, it radiates from within. It ripples out from their very soul outward as it touches others. Everyday people can infect others with their happiness and encourage them to do and live better. If everyone took care of his or her own happiness, then the world would be a much better place.

Every journey described in this book depicts a real person with real circumstances. They were on a path that wasn't making them happy, and they had the courage and inner strength to do something about it. These people have inspired me to make a change, too. I hope that whatever is holding you back from taking that step melts away as you read their "everyday" extra-ordinary, inspirational stories.

Though it's an old cliché, it still holds true: Life is a journey. Decide where you want to go.

ACKNOWLEDGEMENTS

First and foremost, I would like to thank all the courageous souls that contributed their story to this book. You are an inspiration to me, everyone around you, and now the world.

I would like to thank all the planners and doers, the movers and shakers, the optimists and dreamers, and above all, those who believed in us and encouraged us to create the life we love.

1

THE BIG PICTURE

You have the right to pursue happiness. You have the right to live a life you love. You have the right to choose what that is. But, do you have the courage to do it? Do you have what it takes to follow your dreams?

The only reason people are stuck in a life that makes them unhappy is because they are afraid to change it. They have become comfortable being uncomfortable. In this book I'm specifically talking about what you do for a living - your job, your career. Some think, "it's just work - it's something I have to do to survive - I'm not supposed to enjoy it, just do it. I need the money."

Meanwhile, resentment builds, you start getting aches and pains, worry, dread - and all these things that you feel at your job seep into the rest of your life. It affects people around you: friends, family, strangers you meet along the way. All of this results in an unhappy world.

Your job shouldn't make you sick (literally or figuratively). It's a job. It's a way to make a living, but it doesn't have to make you sick in the process. If you're going to be doing something for 40 or more hours a week, 50 or more weeks out of the year, why not make it something you look forward to each day? Why not include it in the life you want to live. Why not create the life you love?

When we're children our imaginations run wild. We have no limits; we dream of being astronauts, magicians, teachers, firemen, actors, singers, etc. It's a shame that. as we grow older, we look at these things as out of our reach.

That couldn't be further from the truth. People are those things, they do these things, so why not you?

Maybe we follow a path that we think we want to pursue, but once we start going down that road, find out it's not what we thought it would be. Sometimes we don't know when to cut our losses and just start over. We stay in a job we hate, and we dig that hole deeper and deeper until we feel there is no way out. Gradually our life becomes unrecognizable to our younger self, who was so full of dreams and ambition. We progressively settle into an unhappy life. The problem with settling is that it doesn't fulfill us, and when we are not fulfilled we are not happy.

It may take one week, 10 years, or longer before we really take a look at ourselves and say, "this isn't what I want to do with my life." Sometimes you know it all along and just don't know how to make that change. The great thing is that every day you are alive is another chance to make a change.

Sometimes we talk ourselves out of our dreams by saying that they're not practical. We ignore the child inside who had a dream of becoming a firefighter or ballerina, we and settle into a path that makes more "practical" sense. It can happen for number of reasons; our parents pushed us towards it, our dream felt a little unrealistic, we didn't have the means to pursue it, or we lack confidence to go forward with it. Whatever the reason may be, we end up settling and suffer as a result. And when we suffer, so does everyone around us.

I don't like to see unhappy people. When people are unhappy, they create a negative ripple effect on others and bring the whole world down with them. I try to do what ever I can to uplift and inspire others to make a change and live a life that will contribute to their happiness.

I began to pay attention and notice that there were people around me who took the leap of faith and went on to live happy fulfilling lives. They had the courage to pursue their dreams and create the life they love. I present their stories to you here in the hopes that you can see for yourself that it is doable - attainable. These people have done it - and yes, you can do it too!

2

Business Owner, Real Estate Broker, Investor, Philanthropist

"Dream big. Believe in yourself. Trust your gut."
~ Gayle Barnes

I am a business owner who holds a Bachelors Degree in Psychology from the University of Southern California. I grew up in San Francisco, CA with my parents and 3 siblings. My parents always worked hard: Dad was in construction, and Mom stayed home to raise the family. After years of saving up, they were able to move all of us into a new home in Sunnyvale, CA - now known as Silicon Valley.

Being a middle-class family, we didn't have enough money to go to a private university. However, through student loans, help from my parents, and a small scholarship, I was accepted by and attended the University of Southern California and proudly graduated with a Bachelors Degree in Psychology. The plan was to move back to the Bay area, find a great job, and eventually start a family of my own. That plan was thwarted when my dad accepted a job on the east coast and the family moved to the Washington DC area. I remained in Southern California and found a great job and started my family here in the Los Angeles area. Things turned out better than expected!

Without a doubt, the most important title I have ever held, however, is "mom." My son is the most important person in my life. He has taught me so many things. If you are a parent you can relate to this! You learn so much from your kids. Sometimes the smallest things can make the most impact.

The Corporate World

Ever since graduating college, I was fortunate enough to be employed at Fortune 500 companies. Everything was going well for me I was happy. I grew up professionally in corporate America and had many successful mentors who helped shape my career and successful climb up the throngs of the corporate ladder to management. I remember pearls of wisdom from many of my executive managers like one at IBM who used to say, "If it wasn't written, it was never said." Or another manager at Kodak who said, "Bet on yourself, go get what you desire." These pearls of wisdom have helped me in different situations throughout my career and still hold true today. I often share them with clients, friends or during speaking engagements to groups of investors, sellers & buyers.

While I was employed at Eastman Kodak - which was a fantastic company to work for - I started to feel like this wasn't what I wanted to do. In the beginning, things had actually worked out very well.

I did a little soul searching and found that real estate was my true passion. The business environment had changed with the digital revolution in filmmaking. As someone who thrives on being a leader and staying on the edge of technology, it was clear that marketing to support young filmmakers at Kodak was no longer relevant. Not wanting to sit on the sidelines and watch the transition from film to digital result in loss of profit and revenue, I decided it was time to take charge of my career and do something that I would be passionate about. After months of soul searching, it became obvious that what I really needed to do was to have my own business working with people who were excited about getting a property for the first time, selling their home to move to a larger one, or selling their first investment property. After all, the marketing programs and customer relationships I built in corporate America would transfer nicely to my own venture.

I planned an exit strategy by dusting off my real estate license, paying for coaching, attending classes and jumping into the real estate industry with both feet. I utilized every dime of retraining dollars that were part of my severance package to get the best training to re-enter the real estate industry. It went off like a bang! I created my brand, launched a marketing campaign and talked with people over the phone for several hours a day. What a payoff! People were so supportive, encouraging, and cooperative. In less than a year, I was helping several people sell their properties. It's been amazing, and I have never looked back! In fact, my first deals in my new business were with clients, former employees and friends that I met in corporate America. How awesome is that? And, even better, we are friends to this day.

Current Success

Today, I am a top producing broker with a client base representing millions of dollars and dozens of the most caring relationships and friendships. I became a broker because I decided it's time to help other agents achieve outstanding levels of success. I also wanted to create a team driven by excellence in serving our clients guided by Christian values. I am in the process of building a team of agents who want to be in the business of building trust. We are not sales people. We connect investors, sellers and buyers with properties that match their goals, and it starts with always trust. Your business is nothing without it.

You see, the same strategies that I learned in corporate America to find, retain and nurture client relationships worked in my business. Of course it didn't happen over night, and I needed funds to launch a successful business. I had to help people make the shift from my corporate background to entrepreneur. But you know what? It was easy for them to do because they always had good experiences with me in the corporate world. They knew my character and trusted me. People!! You have to understand this. You must do good all day, every day. It defines who you are. People will either think of you in a good or bad way when they just hear your name. They have an impression of you, so make it a good one. It will be everlasting if you stay consistent in who you are and what you say you are going to do and deliver every time. Not 9 out of 10. EVERY TIME!!!

Giving Back

I feel it is important to volunteer your time and to give cheerfully and help others. You will feel better about yourself and reap many benefits when you adopt a selfless attitude. It gives me a lot of pleasure to serve as a Board Director for Pomona Valley Habitat for Humanity, Chair the Faith Relations Committee for Habitat and be a member of the Design & Construction Committee for Habitat. I am also a Soroptimist, a member of Christian Business Partners (CBP), Trojan League Associates of the Foothills' and Business Partner Networks (BPN). I also support other organizations including the Diamond Bar Women's Club.

Final Thought

I don't regret leaving the rat race at all, but I do miss having someone else to pay for my health benefits!

Gayle was fortunate enough to have started with a strong foundation. She was clever enough to take what she learned along the way and apply it to where she wanted to go. This is a great example of learning, growing and using the past to create the present, and on to the future. Her journey just goes to show that you don't always need to do a complete 180 to create the life you love.

www.GayleBarnes.com

3

Dream Teacher, Coach, Author

"Dreaming is waking up to your Self."
~ Bonnie Buckner

I am a dreamer, first and foremost. For me, dreaming is about waking up: specifically, waking up to experiences and possibility.

Childhood Dreams

I grew up on a ranch in a small town in remote West Texas. My path started at age three, when I had a nightmare that was, for me, the last in a string of horrible nightmares. There had to be a way to face nightmares instead of being a victim to them! I decided then that I would find a way to understand my dreams and conquer them, and that I would become a teacher of dreaming to help others do the same.

I had two great dreaming teachers during my childhood: my father and my grandmother. They both taught me the two main aspects of dreaming: receiving and manifesting. To receive a dream we must release all expectations, assumptions, judgments, and criticisms. In receiving a dream, we move as we would in prayer – listening, allowing, and dialoguing with this greater aspect of ourselves.

Once, my grandmother woke with the decision to make my Uncle Charles a fruit cake and send it to where he was stationed in the war. She didn't ask why, or put it off – she simply did it upon waking, sending it off with a prayer. When Uncle Charles received the cake he stayed behind at lunch, hiding in his barracks to have it all to himself. The cafeteria was bombed, and my uncle, who had stayed behind, was spared. To my grandmother, dreams were not 'other' – they are here, now, and as much a part of our daily functioning as breathing or a heartbeat.

Receiving a dream means acknowledging them as real and important. Then we must take the dream out and manifest it. Dreaming without action is naught – it is only by manifesting the dream that it becomes reality. But how does one do that?

Listen to Your Passions

Dreams are fueled by the engines of our passions and curiosities and above all the directions of our hearts. As a child, I wanted to be the first female president of the United States, a writer, a psychologist, and a filmmaker. I also hoped to work with other cultures. Above all, I simply wanted to help people. While I knew that I wanted to understand and teach dreaming, I never had any idea that this would be something I could "do" as a career. Somehow this seemed like something to be integrated into the fabric of my everyday life. In remote Texas, I had no real image for a "dream teacher" – that "job" didn't exist!

My father told me to think of my interests as the North Star and to follow them as a sailor would – letting them guide me. Even if I might not touch them with my hands, I would still reach the shore. In school I wrote letters to the President, held student leadership positions, filled notebooks with observations and writings and completed a self-help book, and volunteered in a student Peace Corps program. After college, I turned these all of these interests into careers. I worked in the film industry in various roles including as a writer, co-founded a political-media research firm with high-level campaigns as clients, and co-founded and ran a building restoration company that worked closely with the city in numerous community development projects. I got a PhD in psychology, and I traveled the world. Throughout all of this, carried like a talisman in my pocket, I searched for a dream teacher. I worked with my dreams on my own, and I let my dreams guide me, but I was still wondering: how could I truly learn about dreaming? How could I become a teacher of dreaming?

Direction and Language

Dreams unfold in their own time. Rather than investing us with finality, they give us direction – from there we have to bring them into the world and begin to feel our way toward their fulfillment. That long journey that included what seemed like many labyrinth-like dead-ends through the tangles of my childhood, adolescence, and young adulthood was a necessary part of my development as a dreamer. It was here - in the process, the walking, the unfolding – that I experimented with my dreams. For example, in many instances I would say no to a job that all my mentors and colleagues – once even my father! – were advocating I take but my dreaming inner voice said no. In each of these instances my dreaming showed me the right path for me. And by testing my dreams, trying them out, making decisions based on my dreams, I was learning how dreaming works. Just as Newton dropped many apples to discern the physics of gravity, so must we test again and again our dreaming voice to verify for ourselves their own natural laws.

It is also through these many routes that I gathered the language of my dreaming - the shape and form of it. What does it look like to be a teacher of dreaming? How do I talk about it? With what groups of people do I work? It was here, in the twists and turns, that the image of "job-as-dream-teacher" began to take shape.

Dreaming requires finding a language to express it, and my language derives from my interests and passions – the very things I identified as a child that I have been drawn to in my career life. These passions and interests are the vehicles for expressing and manifesting our dreams.

Dreams Become Reality

Today I teach dreaming to business and creative professionals, social entrepreneurs, inventors, people who work in politics, and for non-profits and NGOs. We meet through the language of our shared passions, and through this language I show them how to use their dreams to unlock their greatest potentials and become who they are meant to be.

It is also through these many paths that I met my dream teacher. One day my dreaming voice was very clear that I should contact a woman, whom I had been introduced to months before in passing as a business connection, and invite her to tea. Having learned to listen to my dreaming voice, and trust it, I did. As perplexed as she was, she arrived at the café to meet me there. I immediately apologized for my distracted demeanor that morning, having woken up from a nightmare. She suggested I tell her the nightmare because she had studied with a great dreaming teacher, and perhaps she could offer insight. A great dreaming teacher! With this link, I soon met this great dreaming teacher and my body came alive - I lit up inside with gold and knew that this was the teacher I have waited my whole life to find. I studied for a decade with her, learning the specific and ancient method of dream work that I now teach.

There is no place to be but right now. At moments in my early life journey, I felt quite distant from my ultimate goal of teaching dreaming. And yet, it was through these very roads that I learned about dreaming and met my dream teacher. It is these very roads that laid the foundation for all the dream teaching I do today. One of the great aspects of dreaming this has taught me is that there is no destination – there is only process. And the process of our unfolding is sacred.

Final Lessons

What are dreams? Dreams are the language of our being – they tell us who we are, our potential, what blocks us, and the way through. We dream at night, and we dream during the day. Dreaming emerges from our bodies, and our bodies show us what works for us and what doesn't, where we are on track and where we've lost touch. Thus, dreaming is about looking within and finding that infinitely unique composition that is Me and bringing it forward to live in the now of waking, tangible life. Following the dreaming path and letting ourselves unfold into our being-ness means a life that often defies the timing that the linear world suggests: career track, marriage track, should's, should nots, and can't's.

Ultimately, dreaming is about selfhood. Do I dare accept that my passions are real and valuable, and do so enough to fully explore them? In spite of all criticisms from myself and others? It is here that our fears arise, and it is through dreams that we can push through them to unfold into our true self. We can look back to our childhood and unearth aspects of ourselves – our passions and interests - we buried in our memory and see how they have inspired us along our path even if we haven't been aware of it. And, having rediscovered them, we can challenge ourselves to 'walk them' – to begin to take a step forward into the expressing of them.

I did finally find a teacher to explain my seminal nightmare from age three – myself. I never told my dream teacher this dream. Instead, using the tools she taught me, I came to understand its message and to make the necessary repairs it was asking me to do. However, the repairs were already in process – the moment we actively engage in dialoging with our dreaming we begin to transform. And as dreaming leads us to non-negotiable self-hood, one finds that, ultimately, we are the ones holding the keys to unlock all our doors.

Bonnie came full circle. She stayed true to her roots and her beliefs, and was able to embrace each step along the way of her journey to create where she is today. She is proof that you can listen to your dreams and follow them to the life you truly were meant to live. She followed her dreams - literally - and came out shining.

www.BonnieBuckner.com

4

Paralegal, Licensed Notary, Dabbling Artist

"If you do what you love or love what you do,
you are bound to succeed."
~ Tina DerHovanessian

I am an immigrant who came to this country 38 years ago as a small child. I didn't speak a word of English and, at an early age, experienced a lot of frustration that was brought on by dealing with culture shock and attempting to assimilate with my new environment and classmates at school. It was a challenge that I'll never forget, but I never gave up. Even back then, failure was not an option for me. Some of the kids were mean, and I experienced my own share of bullying. However, within a few months, I was speaking English fluently and had made friends at school. I went on to graduate junior high and high school with good grades, and was consistently placed in upper division English classes every semester. Then it was off to university, from where I graduated with a bachelor's degree in Marketing.

Now and Then

For the past seven years, I have been working as a corporate paralegal at a law firm in Beverly Hills, California. I have been working in the legal field now for the past fourteen years. Before I went into this field, I worked in the entertainment industry as the executive assistant to the founding partner of a product placement agency. At first, I really liked my job and thought it complemented my marketing degree.

After a couple of years working at that agency, however, I realized it was a dead-end job; there was absolutely no room for advancement. On top of that, I was coming up with some great ideas for pitching new and existing clients, but other employees were stealing my ideas. To make matters even worse, my bosses had begun to take me for granted. They'd always tell me what a great job I was doing, but they had stopped giving me raises due to supposed financial problems with the agency. I knew these problems didn't exist because they kept hiring more people and spending more money on other things. I realized that they were just being cheap with me because they thought I'd never leave. I became very disillusioned with my job and with that industry in general, so in early 2001, I started to search for better opportunities.

Doing This On My Own

Every day, after I got home from work, I would search for new jobs. I used every single resource that was available to me: the internet, newspapers, and trade magazines. I even applied to companies I was interested in that didn't have job openings at the time. I figured it wouldn't hurt to send them a resume, since you never know when things might change and they need to hire someone like you. In February of 2001, opportunity knocked in the form of an unexpected phone call from a law firm recruiter. At first I thought it was a wrong number, because I had purposely avoided applying to ads placed by recruiters. My preference was to pursue direct placement jobs because I didn't want to go through a middle man. However, the caller assured me that I had definitely applied to one of her ads that had been for a marketing position at a law firm. She told me that position had been filled, but she had a Legal Assistant position that she thought I'd be perfect for. I resisted at first. After all, I had no legal experience and found the idea of working with attorneys - in this case, two partners - very intimidating. She told me that they weren't exactly looking for someone with experience in this field. They just wanted someone who was bright with a college degree that they could train from the ground up. After some back and forth, I agreed to meet the two partners, so she scheduled the interview. I figured it couldn't hurt to meet them, even though I didn't think it would lead to anything. Once I did meet them, things went really well. They then asked me back for a second interview, during which they took me to lunch. Within a few days, they gave me an offer to join their firm.

I took a leap of faith and accepted, and I haven't looked back since.

During my time there, I learned a lot and acquired many skill sets ranging from legal assistance to law firm accounting and administration/management. After working there for seven years, I was hired by my present firm in Beverly Hills. My starting position was in their Administration department. I worked as a floater, covering the desks of legal assistants who were out sick or on vacation. Sometimes I would have longer assignments covering legal assistant positions that the firm was trying to fill. While working as a floater, I realized how much I enjoyed doing legal work, and I made the decision to pursue it as a career. In a short amount of time, the firm offered me a full-time legal assistant position, and not long after that, they promoted me to corporate paralegal and provided all the training I needed. I've worked as a paralegal for a few years now and have truly been enjoying it. I am blessed to work with a very smart, talented and pleasant group of attorneys whom I can learn from on a daily basis. I am frequently given new challenges and opportunities for growth, which is very fulfilling. There is so much to learn in this business, and as an ambitious person, I feel that my desires to constantly learn and evolve are finally being met. The sky's the limit!

Inspirations and (Almost) No Regrets

I'm inspired by many people in my life: my father, who is my hero; my longtime friends, who are always there to provide support; and the brilliant attorneys I work with, whom I consider my mentors. I am also inspired by art and music; they excite my senses and sprinkle my life with beauty.

I don't have any major regrets, since I'm happy with my life and believe that everything happens for a reason. However, there are a couple of friends from the past whom I wish I had kept in touch with. I lost contact with them several years ago and have no idea where they are now, but hope that they are happy and doing well.

Tina and her family emigrated from another country. Her courage and determination at a young age has helped her live the American Dream. She and her family rose above the prejudice and bullying to live a life that most of us take for granted. She took a leap of faith into a field that she wasn't familiar with and had not thought of entering into before. She kept an open mind, fell into a career path that was both challenging and fulfilling, and is now living a truly happy life.

5

Mother, Wife, Small Business Owner, Voice Over Artist

"The river always starts by flowing with the landscape, but eventually the river ends up changing the landscape."
~ Kimberly Hebdon

I am a natural-born traveler with roots in many cultures. I was born in Coventry, England, grew up in Cape Town, South Africa, and immigrated to the United States to complete my education. My parents always instilled in me the desire for independence, kindness and generosity. This background has offered me a culturally rich foundation, which has given me a sense of wanting to learn and bring positive change in this world.

My family is of utmost priority to me, and I nourish my close friendships and hold them close to my heart. Nature is my go-to medicine, and laughter is my healer. As an accredited Ayurvedic Wellness Counselor, I dedicate my skills in a relevant and significant way to contribute and commit to assisting my clients to achieve a holistic, healthy lifestyle and to positively transform their lives. I tie this approach into all the work I do, regardless of the industry or who I'm working and interacting with. I am an active campaigner for education, training and enlightenment of all people, and am always happy to assist them in becoming healthier in mind, spirit and body; and also to be more successful citizens of the world.

On My Way

At University, I studied Marketing & Management with the ultimate goal to become a high level Marketing executive. I was always interested in the creative and communication side of marketing, and found my professional career in this field for a B2B Broadcast corporation. After experiencing and being a key member of a number of acquisitions, layoffs, and significant management changes, I began to feel the great pressure of a rather stressful corporate environment. The long hours, tight deadlines, and, in a lot of cases, mismanagement led to be a rather uneasy feeling of knowing that I did not belong in such an environment of stress and chaos. I chose to leave the corporate world and start my own small businesses.

I have been running my own marketing communications business for the B2B realm of Broadcast and professional audio video technology for over 15 years. My clients span the globe and include companies in the US, Germany, Japan, and the UK. While I work on a number of extremely fulfilling projects, and coordinate with many talented people, I often feel overworked and spread too thin across too many activities. I also support a small Natural and Holistic health clinic with their marketing activities, helping them expand their brand and visibility for those seeking a more natural approach to healthcare.

Turning Point

After my son was born, my focus shifted immediately. Work was getting in the way of what had become the most important job of my life - being a mother.

I felt as if I was spinning my wheels working so hard to help small businesses without much time for myself at the end of the day. The financial rewards are no longer a driving priority, as I have now focused my priorities on raising my beautiful little boy and spending time with my husband, family and dear friends. Granted, the financial gains are necessary, however I have a driving emotional shift to focus on what's more important in my life. The juggle between family life and work is a massive feat, and takes constant reminding of what is really important to me at this moment in time.

Creativity Takes the Lead

Recently, I decided a shift in the way I spend my work time would benefit both my family and myself personally. I have often been told that I had a very distinct voice and that I should consider voice over work. This peaked my interest enough to research it. After a few classes, I decided that I really enjoyed it, and started a voice-over business catering to the B2B technology marketplace. Although I still have my foot in marketing communications, I am slowly moving away from that line of work to focus on a creative and more fulfilling career helping small to mid-size businesses expand their brand, with a goal to be a part of their company brand i.e. my voice as their brand.

Getting Here

I made the decision to shift my work focus into voice-over work in 2015. Knowing that it is a very competitive market I knew I may have had the voice, but I did not have the skills. I needed to prepare for this new venture.

I spent 6 weeks in a group voice-over training with about 10 other folks. After learning to use my voice in a number of scenarios, seeing an obvious opportunity, and receiving positive feedback, I decided to work on a series of one-on-one training with an extremely talented and experienced voice-over artist. My training offered me the confidence to work on a professional voice-over demo, which we produced together at the hands of an audio studio in Salt Lake City, Utah. Currently, I'm building my strategy for reaching out to my existing networks to market my voice-over services within the B2B professional technology space.

Right In Front of Me

I had often dreamed of making a major change in my life, doing something different and more rewarding. It was ultimately my son and my husband who gave me the wings I needed. The love I have for them, and the love I receive, opened my heart and mind to new adventures. So now it begins, and so it continues.

When the Time is Right

I regret not following my heart when I was younger. Instead, I had a tendency to follow my brain. I wish that I'd had the emotional maturity to follow my true calling: being independent of corporate chains and balancing my life with less work driven projects, and more change-type projects. But the truth is it often takes many years to reach that maturity and realize one's priorities. So, although one could label this a regret, I think I have come to this moment in my life when I was truly ready, and have gained the proper emotional and professional toolset to make a major shift in my life.

Family has always played an important part in Kimberly's life. Having the courage to try something new to accommodate her desire to spend more time with them brought about a change she might not have pursued as quickly as she did. Change follows desire. Her desire to spend time with her family was her push. Kimberly has literally created a life she loves.

6

Assistant District Attorney

"Education gives you freedom of choice."
~ Keri Herzog

I was fortunate enough to grow up in a loving, supportive environment. My parents taught my brother and I early on to focus and work hard to be the best that we could be.

Now, I am a deputy bureau chief in the Child Abuse & Domestic Violence Bureau in the Suffolk County DA's Office. I'm also the attorney in charge of the Domestic Violence Unit. My responsibilities include supervising a team of lawyers - assigning cases, overseeing courtroom tasks, trials, etc., as well as victim advocates, paralegals, and support staff - I guess you could say I'm kind of like an air traffic controller!

Beginning the Journey

When I entered college I decided to major in English; I loved to read and write and thought it would be a good entry way into becoming a teacher. I didn't decide to become a teacher because I had a passion for teaching; I did it because I thought it was something I could always do just as a job. The problem was that, when I actually did start teaching, I hated every minute of it! It was clear early on that it just wasn't for me.

I was teaching middle school for about three years before I started doing something to change my career path. It was always in the back of my mind; I wanted something more, something else. So I decided to go to school at night.

I have to say, night school was a bit inspiring. The people around me each had their own story of why they were doing it, and they were all different ages and types. They worked, studied & still found time for their spouses and children.

I was about 30 years old, and sometimes juggling both my job and school was challenging. I wasn't sure I could keep doing it. If you could imagine having a full time job in the day, a full class schedule at night, and homework from both work and school, you'd understand the need for a little inspiration. I remember one night in class we celebrated a lady's 50th birthday. I thought to myself, "If she can do it, I can do it, too."

How it Evolved

I entered the graduate degree program and had earned an MA in Counseling & Human Services a year later. During my final semester of graduate school, a college friend recommended me for an unpaid internship in the financial aid office at New York Law School. I began the internship in September; two months later I was offered a position as the assistant director of Financial Aid. I became the director two years later.

Part of my job involved doing on-site inspections of work-study placements. Several students had been placed in district attorneys' offices around the city. As I observed the students, it struck a chord with me - it was love at first sight. I really enjoyed my job in the financial aid office, but I still wanted more. I decided that I would become a lawyer in a district attorney's office.

Getting There

I spoke to my bosses about the possibility of attending law school at night while continuing to work in the financial aid office during the day. At the time, no one had done it before. My bosses were very supportive, going so far as to offer me a reduction in the cost of tuition. I took a class to prepare for the Law School Admission Test, took the test & earned a respectable score. By the time I was in my third year, I realized that I was going to need experience in a law-related job.

A law school friend recommended me for a position as a student legal assistant in the Bronx DA's Office. I'm not saying this to brag, but more to give an example; people are glad to recommend me for positions because they know I am a responsible and capable person. I notice that some people are apprehensive about accepting help from friends and family. But, if you are worth the recommendation, why not accept the help? It makes life a lot easier.

When I decided to leave my job in the financial aid office and accept the position in the Bronx, my income was cut in half. But, in the end, it worked out for me because my experience in the Bronx made me a desirable candidate for the Suffolk County DA's Office. I joined the staff in the fall of 1988, and I've been there ever since. My brief background as a teacher, my masters program, and my supervisory experience in the financial aid office led me to where I am today.

I have to say, I genuinely do not have any regrets: none. Every step I took was for a reason and helped me be better at my job. My background in education helps me with families in crisis, and working in financial aid gave me a strong sense of managing a budget on a large scale. My experiences gave me a lot to bring to the table. I had a real life before becoming a lawyer.

And finally...

Like I mentioned in the beginning, I am fortunate enough to have a supportive family. They took care of me while I was working and going to school. I never had to worry about my basic needs; they kept a roof over my head, fed me, clothed me, not to mention the emotional support and the security I felt knowing that I didn't have to worry about such things. I was able to focus on my goals.

My advice – Be open to the people that are offering you help. I contribute a part of my success to the support of family and friends. I wouldn't be where I am today without them.

Sometimes life takes you on a journey before you find out what you really want to do. Keri kept an open mind knowing that something better had to be around the corner. She wasn't afraid to try new positions or follow other paths. In the end it was her hard work and perseverance that helped her to create a life she loves, but it didn't hurt to let others help her along the way.

7

Librarian, Husband, Father

"Take responsibility for yourself…
In life, you can either take a chance or fail to advance."
~ Herb Mendelson

I am a man in my eighties who is married to a wonderful supportive woman, and I am blessed to have two great children and three amazing granddaughters. I live in New York in the house that my wife grew up in. I am a depression-era baby, so my mindset has always been about living modestly and making the best of what I have: which may be the reason why I waited so long before deciding to make a change in my career. I also have many hobbies that include reading, singing, exercising, and learning languages.

At this point, I am what you would call "semi-retired." Although I officially retired from two jobs over the course of my lifetime, I am still working part-time as a Librarian in a neighboring town's library. I enjoy doing this kind of work because it allows me to help adults and children face-to-face every day. When I am not at the library, I take care of one of my granddaughters, which is a job in itself but extremely rewarding.

Starting Out

My story has a tortured past. When I graduated high school, I did not have the desire to study and had no real idea what I wanted to do with my life. As a result, I joined the United States Navy: mainly because of the opportunities the armed services offers. After boot camp, I was assigned to work as a Yeoman, or clerk typist, in the personnel department on a ship.

Unfortunately, after five years of military service, I still had not figured out what I wanted to do for a living. My father insisted that I either go back to school or learn a trade. He had a brother who was connected with the men's garment union and he was able to get me a job working in that industry, so I decided to try it out. It seemed like the easier of the two choices. After five years of working at that trade, I knew that I had to do something else. I hated every minute that I spent at that job. One day, I visited a friend of mine who was working in a beauty salon. I decided that I would give the beauty industry a try. I went back to beauty school and obtained employment with a leader in the hairdressing industry in their corporate offices in Manhattan. I enjoyed the work tremendously and received accolades as technical training manager running their training center, but my prospects were dismal because, although I tried to improve my status in the company, promises of opportunities were made to me that were never fulfilled.

Frustrations

The executives made false promises to me that I would to move up in the company if I got a college degree. The only problem was that I was a 35 year old married man with two young children. Hoping for the best, I spoke to my wife about my situation and, with her support, I applied to night school and was accepted. When I started college, I was 37 years old. My day started at 5:00 A.M. My transportation consisted of taking trains between my apartment in Brooklyn, my job in Manhattan, and my school in New Jersey. I worked all day in Manhattan, and went to school at night in New Jersey, most evenings getting home somewhere between midnight and 1:30 A.M. several times a week. At 46 years old, I achieved a Bachelors Degree in Vocational Education.

Despite all of my hard work, the promises of a higher position within the company never came to fruition. Instead, my bosses kept me in the position of technical training manager because, according to them, I was skilled at this job and they did not want to move me and have to find a replacement for that position. Oddly enough, these same executives had friends within the industry who they brought in to fill vacant positions that I had hoped to be placed in. I knew that I had to do something. I realized that, despite my best efforts, the higher-ups were still trying to keep me stagnant. I was so miserable that my job was beginning to affect my personal life. After dealing with disappointment, frustration, and company politics, I knew that I needed to change my situation.

A Change for the Better

At this point, I was a 53 year old man with teenage children who realized that he needed a whole new career. My wife was a Librarian at the time and was very happy with her career choice. She was able to help people and had a better working environment. I decided to go back to school to get my Masters Degree in Library Science. With my wife's full support, I applied and was accepted to Library school. Again, my day began at 5:00 A.M. I used different modes of transportation to commute between our new apartment in Brooklyn, my job in Manhattan, and my school on Long Island. This time, I went to school at night and on weekends. I worked all day in Manhattan, and school at night on Long Island several nights a week. Most evenings, I would get home somewhere around midnight.

At 58 years old, I achieved a Masters Degree in Library Science. After graduating, I retired from the corporate world and secured a position as a reference Librarian in a public library. You can not imagine how relieved and satisfied I was when I got to tell my bosses in the beauty industry that I was leaving. I even made sure to tell them why I was leaving and exactly what I thought about their tactics. For the first time in my life, I found my niche ... as a Librarian. I loved my work, and my employer, as well as the patrons, appreciated me. After working an additional 13 years as a full time Librarian, I finally retired at 70 years old. At 84 years old, I am currently employed part-time as a Librarian in the same library that I retired from. Helping people find what they are looking for gives me great satisfaction.

Inspirations and Regrets

Besides the negativity at work, I recognized that I had to have the strength to move forward with my life and make a better situation for myself. I also understood that things would improver for me if I accomplished my goals. Of course, I could not have done any of this without my wife's support and encouragement.

I do regret that it took so long for me to find myself, and that I did not pursue an education until later in life. I also wish I had not waited so long before leaving a situation that was stagnant and made me miserable.

"Take responsibility for yourself. Even though it appears that others are holding you back, be mindful that when others stand in your way, they are the necessary motivation to propel you to where you want to be. In life, you can either take a chance or fail to advance."

Herb's story is one of determination and perseverance. He would not give up for his chance at happiness. Every time he started down a path that wasn't working for him, making him and his family unhappy, he chose to try again, and again, until he found the life he loved. His story is a reminder to try and try until you find it…your happy place.

8

Attorney, Social Worker

"Sometimes the most painful things result in the greatest growth, fulfillment and joy."
~ Susan Onorato

When I graduated from college in the late 70's, I was drawn to two different career paths: law and psychology. I chose the latter for two reasons: I wanted to avoid the statistics course that was required for a psychology Masters, and I knew that ultimately a Doctorate (with thesis) would be required to engage in private practice. I wasn't exactly enamored with the idea of the cost or length of such a post-graduate education.

After making my decision, I applied to multiple law schools, and was actually accepted by several. I was quite disappointed that I did not make it into my first choice and alma matter, Fordham University. Still, I embraced the more affordable Brooklyn Law School. The only field I wanted to work in was sex crimes prosecution. I had volunteered at a Rape hotline in college, and felt strongly about the epidemic. I wanted to be a part of the solution.

I both enjoyed and suffered through the three years of law school and upon graduation with my J.D. degree; I attempted to get a job in a metropolitan area District Attorney's Office. Eventually I did get that job, and I immediately volunteered for the Sex Crimes Bureau, which was not as popular as it is today in the era of "Law and Order." I thrived, trying and winning difficult cases. Unfortunately, there came a time when office politics overrode my passion for helping victims and stopping the bad guys. Even worse, the bureau was eventually dismantled. Needless to say, I left.

Eye Opener

Moving on, I went into the field of medical malpractice defense. Initially I hated it, but grew to like being one of the few female trial attorneys in the field at that time, and I liked making more money. I did miss doing justice for victims, but for the most part I found justice and fulfillment in representing those fine medical professionals and institutions that had been frivolously sued.

After much hard work, I became partner. At the time, I had no idea that basically meant handing over my soul! At one point, my father became extremely ill and was on his deathbed. I wanted to be there for him, to visit my dying father, and I was "forbidden." That was just too much - it crossed a line. The time requested was four days over Memorial Day weekend! How could they deny me that? It was clear to me that the experience pointed up the disparity between a female partner and the males. I was told unabashedly that the "boys" had a golf outing to attend, so I must handle a "women's issue case"— alleging failure to diagnose breast cancer. Wow - a brief adjournment could have been easily obtained. This made it impossible to ignore that my partnership was nothing more than a name to them.

I really started to miss my job in prosecution, so I decided to go back. Unfortunately, it all ended abruptly for me in 2007. I was suffering from truly disabling menopause, and the macho environment of law enforcement was not a friendly one. I mention this because although viewed as a "women's" issue characterized by relatively benign manifestations such as hot flashes and moodiness, (the butt of many jokes), my symptoms included depression, crippling insomnia, and anxiety in court, a phenomenon never before experienced. I was even struggling with word retrieval; which was quite frustrating as I had always been know to be very articulate. None of this is to suggest that all women suffer similarly, but I have to tell my story authentically.

I knew that I was in trouble when I confided in my boss, who was several years younger, and as I wept in embarrassment and naked vulnerability he said, "What makes a hormone? Not paying her." It was crushing, but no longer surprising, to be mocked and marginalized despite all of the medical documents I had shown him. Of course the reason given for this humiliating termination was incompetence, with plausible deniability of the true situation. As I was escorted from the building by friendly detectives embarrassed to be so tasked they comforted me, the female detective whispered, "don't let them see you cry" as we walked out. The male detective said, "Whenever a door closes a window opens," and I quipped ruefully that I'd like to jump out off it. Humor and dignity carried the day for me. They always have.

Moving On

What followed was a long period of soul-searching and trying volunteer opportunities in related fields. Still, I felt unfulfilled and diminished since I had defined myself as a career professional for so long.

Around that time, I had become involved in community resources offering a path to recovery for people struggling with addiction. I had family members who were afflicted and wanted to learn healthy coping skills. This practice completely changed the trajectory of my life.

I explored the possibility of becoming a therapist, but the academic avenue through which to accomplish this goal was at first elusive. It seemed as if the most appropriate approach would be to obtain a Masters in Social Work so I could practice counseling as an LMSW. I went to a couple of open houses hosted at various nearby universities, but was overwhelmed by the cost and number of years required to hang out a shingle, which is what I thought I wanted to do. The LCSW required many years of post-Masters clinically supervised hours followed by an additional licensing exam, and I wasn't getting any younger. The Social Work program at Stony Brook University was suggested to me for its academic excellence and affordability. I was hesitant to jump in due to a combination of fear and reluctance, so I took a couple of courses to test the waters. I found them both rewarding and challenging, and applied for admission. For me, the application process was a challenge as it was all online. Although I had amassed a modicum of computer savvy, I was overwhelmed by the rigidity of the format. So I took the process one step at a time, reinforcing my confidence, and was admitted some months after submitting the lengthy application.

Surprisingly, I found the program more challenging than I had law school. Some opined that it was a function of my age, but I don't think so. I persevered, and ironically even scraped through the required Statistics course I had so assiduously avoided all those years ago. A kindly, patient, brilliant professor coaxed me over the finish line.

After graduation, the next hurdle was sitting for the licensing exam. Although there was much hype, with the help of a "boot camp," my friends and I passed. (This too was an entirely computerized event at a test-taking site, but by this time I was almost proficient.)

During my matriculation at Stony Brook, I had the opportunity to intern at a mental health facility catering to a population of people without the means to engage in costly therapy, and at a center for recovery from addiction. I loved both, but was more drawn to helping those struggling with addiction. The program is what is known as Twelve-Step based, and after a few years, has become my home as I've answered my calling.

I love working with people who are trying to recover from the devastating effects of addiction. I view this work as both a gift and a privilege.

Some people remark on how different my former occupation is from my present one, but I beg to differ. I practiced social work every time I helped a victim through the process of getting justice, and also worked for justice and dignity for those accused.

Lastly...

I really have no regrets. I don't believe in them. As cliché as it may sound, I truly feel as if everything happens for a reason.

Finally, my stepdaughter was my greatest inspiration. In her practical, confident way she urged me to go for social work. So, as a special 'thank you,' I gave her my gold tassel from graduation.

Susan's journey had two paths that appealed to her and took one that made more sense to her at the time. The 1st path lead her back to the 2nd in a more profound way. Susan needed to take that course to become the person she needed to be for the life she has created now. We're all works in progress and the key is to keep moving forward. Susan did, and is now living a fulfilling life she loves.

9

Creative Entrepreneur

"Learn from your mistakes, be kind, and move on."
~ Christine Purse

I am a wife and mother of twin girls, now in college, and have worked in the entertainment industry for over 25 years. I founded ignite strategic communications, which offers skilled and thoughtful strategy to help our clients with their business and professional goals, eleven years ago in Los Angeles, CA. ignite has grown from a part-time assistant, one client, and me to an elite staff of colleagues with an enviable client list.

Following Passion

After college, I went right into the healthcare profession. From an ad in the paper, I got an incredible opportunity to work on the launch of a progressive gerontology center in my hometown of Denver, CO. Since the services there were integrated across disciplines, a new concept at the time, I had the chance to work with the hospital's team in setting up the Health Center from the ground up. Luckily, I got to set up the community outreach to seniors, and community education for the neighborhood. I loved it. It was an incredible experience and I got to interact with a broad range of people, from legislators, activists, doctors, neighborhood residents, and seniors. It was deeply rewarding to see how we impacted the lives of our patients.

Though I enjoyed my job, I came to a crossroads when I started graduate school in public administration. That would have sent me on the healthcare management path, for good. Deep down, I knew that unless I nurtured my creative side, I might regret it. I had always been interested in movies and documentaries and wanted to be a part of that world.

Four years after changing course, working at a PBS station, a commercial production company and finally an advertising agency, I made a decision. While at the agency

I produced a PSA for the Children's Museum of Denver that won a regional Emmy, a SAG award, and a number of other honors. That gave me the courage to take a leap of faith, and apply to the American Film Institute (AFI). I got accepted, packed up everything and moved to Los Angeles. It was terrifying, but remains one of the best decisions of my life. I launched a career as a filmmaker and never looked back.

Added Bonus

Not only did I move forward with my film career, but I also met my husband at AFI. He was enrolled in their screenwriting program. His first project was to write a script, and mine was to produce. I chose to produce his script because it was clearly the best! From then on, we became a team - both professionally and personally.

After we graduated from AFI, we launched a production company - Echorock. Echorock made music videos, commercials, and an independent feature, "Friends and Enemies."

Three or four years into filmmaking, it seemed as if the job didn't fit; working on the production and development side just wasn't for me. I also wanted a steady income since we were thinking of starting our family.

A Chain Reaction

Through Echorock, I had been working at LaserPacific Media - a progressive, inventive, and very exciting post production facility in Hollywood, CA. When I let my intensions of joining the workforce be known, I was asked to join the team at LaserPacific. That proved to be a game-changing opportunity for me, and I opened their account services division (in-house producers).

I watched the industry rapidly evolve, and LaserPacific was at the vanguard of those changes. Working there allowed me to be part of a company that was one step ahead of some of the most exciting technologies that create motion pictures, television and other media content.

I found my tenure at LaserPacific to be exciting, and challenging. I was never bored, not even for one day. Often, I had to completely stretch to understand the technology landscape. All the while, the entrepreneur in me wanted to see if I could do something on my own, something new, something different.

One afternoon, while sitting in a screening with a customer and her publicist, the idea ignited (pun intended). The publicist was older, very successful, and he didn't have any idea why all of the things that were going on were really, really exciting. It was at that moment that it clicked for me; I saw an opportunity to articulate the message that technology enables storytellers.

I realized there were people and companies responsible for bringing us the entertainment, which we all enjoy, that were going under appreciated. It was clear that there was going to be much more technological advancement, not less, and I wanted to be part of that end of the business, to bring those stories to the forefront. I also perceived that it was a good opportunity; there were not that many expert communicators in entertainment technology at that time. That's obviously changed since then. We now have great competition, which is a good thing!

Taking the Steps

My mother played a big part in my decision to start my own company. I watched her build a great business in Denver as a real estate developer and agent in a time when women didn't really have big careers. On top of that, she was always a wonderful mother and homemaker at the same time. She was bright, beautiful, funny, and actually cared about her customers. Many people were able to get their houses, stores and offices, because she persevered. She went the extra mile and made it happen for them. And, all the while, she was there for us. Throughout it all, she had the support of a wonderful partner: my dad. He didn't want to hold her back, he wanted her to fly. Her life and their relationship encouraged me and gave me inspiration.

Before I resigned from my job, I took the time to think through a simple business plan. I gave it critical thought and visualized who my clients would be; who would hire me. I had a significant list before I gave my resignation because I gave it the time and consideration that such a bold move truly deserved.

During the lead up to handing in my resignation, (while still performing at my job), I took every lunch, dinner and event as an opportunity to meet and connect with journalists, potential customers, and creative people. Planning was important. The day I resigned I had already opened an office, had my own phone number, logo, web address, and business cards.

Every industry is its own "small world," and relationships are critical. That's why I always nurture mine. I try to be meticulously honest, and don't believe in ever, ever burning a bridge. Because of my work ethic, my former employer became my first client. We already had a relationship, and I built upon that trust and insight to make it happen. I continue to work with him today as he has moved on in his career.

Being Grateful

So far my life has been a wonderful ride. When asked if I have regrets - sure I do, but I'm not dwelling on them and don't think it's good to re-live them. I try to learn from my mistakes, be kind, and move on. I love this quote by Douglas Adams, "I may not have gone where I intended to go, but I think I have ended up where I needed to be." I believe it's important to think about that anytime life takes you where you never thought you'd go.

I just have to add; professionally, I've been blessed to live in a time of such dynamic technological advancement. I run a business with an incredible group of people. My colleagues at ignite are the best there is, and it's an honor to work with them, day in and day out. Our clients - not kidding - are among the smartest people on the planet and they constantly impress me. There is a lot of "how did you DO THAT!" in our customer's inventiveness. It's exciting to have to focus and listen carefully, because what they are working on is complex, creative, and important in our sector of business.

More than all of that, however, is that I somehow have a really, really wonderful family, which I almost feel like I don't deserve. If that were all I'd gotten from this experience, it would have been more than enough!

Chris always listened to her heart and followed its lead. It is said that in life there are no coincidences, and she paid attention to universal messages. It's a chain reaction; because she decided to do what she loved, others were able to join her on her journey and be a part of the business she created, which helped others create the life they love.

ignite.bz

10

Police Officer, Husband, Father

"Anything is possible
if you set your mind to doing something."
- Jeff Toscano

I am a law enforcement professional in my forties who is married to an attorney. We live in New York, in a home we own, with our two and a half year old daughter and three dogs. I enjoy watching sports, boxing, lifting weights, and getting tattoos. In my thirties, I changed my life by leaving a career in the financial industry to become a police officer. Since doing this, I have had the opportunity to work as a patrol officer and, for the last several years, as a plainclothes officer who is assigned to a unit that is dedicated to proactive policing. Even though I work long hours in a rotating shift and deal with demanding and dangerous situations, I know that I am helping people and protecting the public.

I am a plainclothes police officer working the night shift in a special unit within our precinct. I am assigned to do proactive policing: a process that discourages crimes through our show of police presence and engaging the public to better understand their concerns in an effort to alleviate them. I still dabble in finance by giving my family and friends financial advice, and I also handle my immediate family's finances by paying bills, investing, and setting up a "nest egg."

Wall Street

I was a sales trader in the finance industry who worked in a financial institution on Wall Street. I commuted to and from work every day from Long Island to New York City by the Long Island Railroad. Despite my hard work, things were not going the way I had hoped. There never seemed to be any opportunities for advancement and no assurances for job security, given the state of the economy and the politics that were rampant within the company that I worked for. To make things worse, my bosses never fully appreciated me or followed through with the promises that they made. Instead, they just piled on more responsibilities without any additional compensation or a promotion. Every day, I was becoming more and more dissatisfied with this work and felt as if I wasn't really contributing to society in any meaningful way.

What I Wanted

I decided that I had to have the courage to change the course of my life and do what I wanted to do, rather than what others had expected of me. As far back as I can remember, I wanted to be a police officer. It was my dream career, but my parents and the rest of my family did not support my choice of career. They pressure on me to take a job that they believed was more valued, more respected, and more mainstream. Because I wanted to please them, I chose the wrong path for me. I went into the finance industry half-heartedly, but I worked hard and was an exemplary employee once I was there. I figured I might as well make the best of it and do the best job that I could. Unfortunately, being a motivated, hard worker and doing a good job was apparently getting me nowhere in that profession, and I was certainly feeling as though something was missing for me personally.

When I decided to do what was right for me and make a career change to become a law enforcement professional, I was recently married to my first wife. Prior to our engagement, I had informed my fiancé that I had always wanted to be a police officer and that I might pursue that avenue. She was not supportive of my potential career change and seemed to think that I would never have the courage to make that move. Ultimately, she was wrong; I did have the courage.

Not surprisingly, this decision ended my marriage because, like my family, my first wife wanted me to continue in the finance industry because she thought it held a certain status.

I've always had good experiences with the police officers I've met over the years, and was drawn to all of their positive portrayals in television series and movies. There was also a very strong desire to look out for the health and safety of the public. Of course, I also understood that I could not continue the job I had indefinitely, since I was so miserable. To this day, I wish that I had made that career change sooner. When I finally dove into it, I was already in my thirties.

Making the Change

I started off by talking to police officers about the job to learn more about what it entails. I then got myself into prime physical shape (through working out and eating properly), studied test police test preparation manuals, and took several of the exams. Once at the Police Academy, I applied myself to all of my studies: both academic and physical training. Throughout this entire process, I was sure to give it all of the respect it deserves. Once I finally left the academy and was on the job, I worked hard to be the best I could be every day.

I would also like to report that, after becoming a police officer, I met my current wife during the course of my duties at work; she is an attorney. I'm happy to say that she is totally supportive of my job and, even better, understands its rigors.

My Dream Come True

Since graduating from the Police Academy I have had the opportunity to help people in the following ways:

1. Make split second decisions that have saved lives, including my own.
2. Assist sick and injured persons.
3. Mediate disputes.
4. Diffuse volatile situations.
5. Recover stolen vehicles.
6. Take dangerous felons off of the street.
7. Recover large amounts of dangerous drugs.
8. Recover unlicensed weapons (some of which have been used in violent crimes).
9. Assist in locating fugitives and persons with a warrant for their arrest.
10. Assist detective squads in solving cases.
11. Assist other specialized units (such as narcotics, vice, bureau of special operations) during the course of their assignments.
12. Assist with security details when entertainers or high-level politicians are in town.
13. Lecture at schools about the importance of staying on the right path.

Currently I am working for the Bureau of Special Operations, which is comparable to the SWAT Team. I have been involved in several extremely dangerous situations, but, at the end of the day, knowing that I risked myself to protect others from harm is rewarding. I definitely made the right choice to follow my dreams.

"If a person digs deep within themselves, they will find their own strength and determination to accomplish their goals. Change is scary, but taking the leap towards happiness is never a wrong move. You have to be true to yourself. Stick with your dreams and make them a reality. Anything is possible if you set your mind to doing something."

Jeff tried to please his family with his original career choice. He wasn't happy with his "chosen" path and had no support, not even from his first wife, to pursue his dream. Thankfully, his passion to be a police officer was strong, and his dream did not die. He was able to come out from under others expectations and pursue his true calling. He had the courage to make the move and do what he really wanted to do. Now he has a wife that supports him and is living his dream.

11

Law Professional, Wife, Mother

"...be your own personal hero."
~ Sondra Toscano

I am a career woman who is married to a law enforcement professional. We live in a modest home on Long Island, New York with one precious little girl and three adorable puppies. I made the decision to change my life by returning to school and pursuing a law career. Since graduating with a Juris Doctorate, I have completely devoted myself to public service. I am a hard worker with strong ethics who takes pride in being a civil servant.

Right now, I am a court attorney to a family court judge. I am responsible for preparing written decisions and memorandums of law on complex legal issues arising in court cases. To that end, I am also responsible for researching the law, analyzing case facts, and applying the law to these facts after consulting with my boss regarding our cases. Additionally, I am in charge of scheduling and conducting conferences towards settlement, or readiness for trial. In the context of my job, I handle cases involving child abuse and neglect, custody and visitation, and juvenile delinquency, as well as adoptions when those types of cases are interwoven with the child protective matters to which my boss is assigned. Although it is stressful work and deals with many sensitive and difficult issues, I know very well that I am making a positive difference in people's lives.

After establishing myself in a career and starting a family, I began to reconnect with songwriting, which I had been creating before deciding to go to law school. I relearned to play the guitar, and started to write songs again. Songwriting is a fabulous outlet for my creative side, which has always been an integral part of me. It allows me to positively affect peoples' lives through music and words. Since my daughter was born, she has always had my appreciation for music. Now that I have achieved success in the legal profession,

I am pursuing a music career again. Having gained legal knowledge, I am more focused, more knowledgeable, and better prepared than ever.

At First...

Before entering the legal world, I was vocalist, songwriter, and entertainer pursuing a career in the music business while working as an administrative employee at a Jewish temple. My music career was not progressing in the manner I had envisioned, and my administrative job was low paying and had no chance for advancement or any opportunities to blossom into a decent career.

The list of reasons for why I was unhappy with my job at the temple was endless. The money I was making did not match my intellect and abilities. I did not feel valued, was not challenged, and felt like my life was on cruise control. To put it simply, I knew I wasn't meeting my full potential. Day after day, I couldn't help but feel as if there was something better in store for me.

Heading to Law School

I finally realized that I am the master of my own domain, that I could not expect things to get better unless I took actions to improve my life. I started by researching financial assistance to help pay for my college expenses. I went back to school to finish my undergraduate degree at Long Island University (C.W. Post Campus), where I ultimately received a Bachelor of Arts in Criminal Justice. While there, I was on the Dean's List and I joined several honor societies. I graduated with a perfect grade point average and won several academic awards.

While finishing my undergraduate degree, I applied, and was accepted, to several law schools. I ultimately chose Hofstra University School of Law after being offered a merit scholarship as an incentive. I was awarded a Charles H. Revson Law Students Public Interest Fellowship Grant and, once again, made the Dean's List.

Since I knew that I wanted to be a litigator, I took courses applicable to litigation. This included clinical programs, such as the criminal justice clinic and the National Institute for Trial Advocacy trial techniques program. Since I was a little older than the other students, I ended up taking many of them under my wing. I also joined the Phi Alpha Delta International Law Fraternity and became their representative during my first year of law school.

Because I knew that I wanted to work in public service, I interned in public service organizations during law school. These included the Nassau County Police Department in their Legal Bureau and the United States Attorney's Office for the Eastern District of New York's Central Islip location. In this way, I was able to gain valuable knowledge by assisting lawyers who were working in areas that were of interest to me.

Even though law school was extremely time-consuming and overwhelming, and there were many times when I wanted to quit, I would not let myself be swayed from my goals. I stayed focused and applied myself to my studies. I ultimately graduated in the top of my class with a Juris Doctorate. At graduation, I was awarded the Hofstra University Clinical Law Courses Award.

Highlights of My Career

After graduating from Hofstra School of Law, I accepted a two-year position as a law clerk to the Honorable Steven M. Gold in the United States District Court for the Eastern District of New York. This was a hybrid position in which I also served as Magistrate Gold's courtroom deputy.

After my temporary assignment with Judge Gold ended, I secured a position with the Suffolk County District Attorney's Office, where I commenced and prosecuted criminal cases in both trial and investigative bureaus. During that time, I represented the People of the State of New York in numerous hearings and trials. I also conducted long-term, complex criminal investigations. During the course of the investigations, I dealt with confidential information and a team of various levels of rank within a myriad of law enforcement organizations. While working for the Suffolk County District Attorney's Office, I was cross-designated as a Special Assistant United States Attorney for the Eastern District of New York under the "Project Safe Neighborhoods" initiative, where I prosecuted violations of Federal firearms laws. While I was cross-designated, I carried two concurrent caseloads, one as a state prosecutor and one as a Federal prosecutor.

After working as a Federal and state prosecutor, I obtained a position with the Nassau County Attorney's Office where I defended civil rights claims. There, I had a caseload of labor-intensive civil actions to which I was assigned and was responsible for litigating. As a government civil litigator, I was required to investigate and assess each case assigned to me. Again, I dealt with confidential information as well as co-counsel, support staff, and a variety of levels of rank within a myriad of law enforcement organizations. Where, as a prosecutor, I had always considered the defense position in my analysis of cases and strove to seek justice, my understanding of the defense position, during this time, crystallized. Being a defense attorney allowed me to form a new perspective on cases and turned me into a much more tempered litigator.

While working in the Nassau County Attorney's Office's General Litigation Bureau, I requested a transfer to the Family Court Bureau. When I was transferred there, I represented out-of-state custodial parents and their children pursuant to the Uniform Interstate Family Support Act. I also represented the Nassau County Department of Social Services to recoup public assistance funds. I litigated issues revolving around paternity, spousal support, and child support. Since Family Court deals with human emotions within their fact patterns, it was at this point in my career where I dealt with the most difficult clients and adversaries under unique and challenging circumstances. I was assigned clients who were emotionally and mentally exhausted, impassioned to the point of distraction, and championing for their position without reason. Then there were the adversaries, oftentimes self-represented, who were volatile, severe, and unbending. My time spent there further increased my ability to calm frustrated litigants and diffuse embroiled situations.

I then accepted a position as the Court Attorney to the Honorable Barbara Salinitro. This was immediately prior to her part becoming the first of what would be several trial parts in Queens County Family Court, which offer immediate trials and were formulated to facilitate speedy resolutions in cases. As the initial trial part court attorney, I was responsible for both administrative and legal work towards its functionality. In February 2015, Judge Salinitro and I were transferred to Kings County Family Court where we are currently assigned to one of the trial parts. In Kings County Family Court, I am responsible for research, writing, and conferencing cases. Such an arrangement provides an environment for me to interact with litigants and attorneys in an equally meaningful way, but from a slightly different perspective, than I had been in Queens County Family Court.

Inspirations and Regrets

Ultimately, I decided that I was tired of being average and that I wanted to make a difference. Since most of us spend the bulk of our waking hours at work, it was crucial for me to be fulfilled by my job. I had parents with strong work ethics who stressed to me the importance of education and being the best that I could be. My parents were entirely supportive of my goals and were my cheerleaders.

I do regret, however, that I didn't have the proper focus and application when I was younger and that I didn't make a change sooner. I also regret that I took a hiatus from songwriting when I clearly could have incorporated both my music and my studies into my life instead of feeling that I had to give up one for the other. You truly can have it all. And now that I know this, I'm in the process of reviving my music career.

At the end of the day, I know for sure that my legal career has allowed me to positively impact people's lives by helping them to manage difficult situations. I truly am a part of a process that is exceptionally rewarding.

"You have to truly want to change. If you want to change, you can change. You have to set your intention and commit yourself to making that change. You have to make it happen by being certain that it will and taking the necessary steps without being afraid of change, or failing. If you don't put it out into the universe, the answer will always be no, but if you do put it out into the universe, then the answer can be yes. So formulate your goals, stick to them, and make them happen. Be your own personal hero."

Sondra took an honest look at where she was in her life and realized that it wasn't going the way she had hoped. Instead of staying on that path and ending up miserable and bitter, she chose to take responsibility for her future. She was determined and chose to take control of her life. She planned and created goals to achieve a life that has been rewarding and fulfilling.

bigcitycowgirl.com
facebook.com/bccg72/

12

Systems Developer/IT, Professional Poker Player, DJ/Producer

"There is always more then one way to accomplish something. Success is not linear."
~ Jaywill Sands

I grew up "in the hood" of Los Angeles. My parents divorced when I was about three. My mom was a busy secretary at Motown, and I was a latchkey kid. I first went to Virginia Road Elementary School (Adams & Jefferson) and would get into fights all the time. It was a rough school and I was bullied a lot. It got so bad that the kids would even come to my house to pick fights!

Thankfully, my mom saw what was going on and took me out of public school. She enrolled me in Area E Alternative School, which got me away from all the rowdy kids and put me in a more positive environment. It also took away the fear of going to school. Things seemed to be going really well for us. It was early in 1975, during sixth grade, when my class went on a field trip to JPL. That was a highlight in my life. We saw a prototype of the first Viking Lander, and my passion was born. Right then, I decided I wanted to be an astrophysicist.

Tragedy

On June 2nd 1975, everything changed for the worse. On that day, my mother was murdered, and I was the unlucky one who discovered her body. I was only ten years old at the time. The same year I realized my dream to become an astrophysicist is the same year it was squashed because I lost my mother.

I remember that day so clearly, too. I kissed my mom in the car after she dropped me off at school that morning. At nutrition time, I played a game of baseball with the other kids. I was up at bat and hit the baseball over the parking lot fence, which was eighteen feet high across the field! That wasn't normal. Everybody was stunned that a ten-year-old could do that.

After school, I got off the RTD bus and, as I was walking home on the block where I lived, I looked seven or eight houses down and saw that my mom's car was parked in the driveway. I thought she must have gotten off work early. I was so excited to see that she was home. That feeling of warmth that a boy has for his mom on a wonderful, sunny day was like walking down the yellow brick road for me!

A therapist would later point out that it was one of the last happy moments of my childhood. The day that my mom died, everything stopped; my passion, my family, everything I knew and loved was gone.

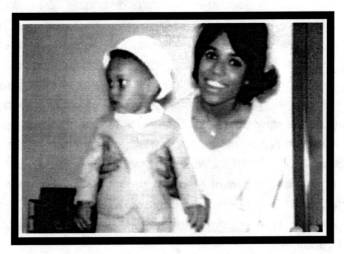

I went to live with my father and stepmother, who had three children together: my sister and two brothers. My stepmother was exactly what you'd expect: an evil stepmother just like in Cinderella. I never had the chance to grieve over the death of my mother or to heal from the trauma. There was no compassion, no tenderness, just a lot of psychological abuse from my step-mom. Looking back, I really feel that I grew up without a mother.

To make matters worse, I was forced to grow up without my mother's side of the family. My father and mother always had such a volatile relationship with different views on religion; she was a Jehovah's Witness, and he was an atheist.

Almost Famous

It wasn't until many years later that I knew I had to do something with my life. The music business peaked my interest. And I decided to pursue that full-time.

I eventually became an award-winning DJ, and simultaneously was in a well-respected local rap group with a record deal - The Shake City Rockers. We were the first Hip Hop crew in Los Angeles, est. 1979, which spawned my interest in music production. We were also the first rap group ever signed to Motown records... long story short, they closed their doors two months later. My music career evolved into producing, and I was part of a company called Shake City Productions. We had some pretty talented artists on-board, and a few of them even received major record deals. It felt like fame and fortune were right around the corner... except that corner kept turning another corner, and then another.

I love music, and I always have, but music didn't pay the bills. Eventually, I found myself homeless, sleeping in the studio, and then started living out of my car. Things got even worse when my car was towed.

Besides the obvious reasons for why things weren't going well, I noticed that everyone I worked with - my manager, co-producers, and even my artists - all had regular jobs. They were able to keep a roof over their heads and food in their stomachs while I was sleeping in my car. I had sacrificed everything because I believed I had to.

When you're young, it's easier to go with the flow because certain things, like stability, don't seem as important. But once you start to mature, suddenly a couch isn't enough. I looked back and saw what was really going on in my life. I had a revelation - I wasn't being treated fairly and became frustrated and angry. Something had to give. I needed to start thinking about me for once.

When you're in the moment, you don't really see the reality of what's going on. It's not until you step away for a bit that you can see clearly. Things weren't working out, and I wasn't living the life I wanted to live. I can still pinpoint the exact moment that I decided to make a change:

I was living in my car at the time. After another all night music session, I drove over to North Hollywood and parked over by a paint and body shop to sleep. It was summer and I knew that when the sun came up it would be in a shaded area. I was fast asleep when I heard a knock at my window. It was a worker from the shop. He came to tell me that they were about to open and that I couldn't sleep there. At that point, I knew I'd had enough.

A Turning Point

Just when I needed it, I received $1800 came from selling one of the music programs I created. And that's when my life started to turn around. It was just enough money to rent a tiny basement apartment and have a little left over for food for the rest of the month. It wasn't the nicest place; I remember the biggest, black water bugs I had ever seen would start crawling under door at dusk. But at least I wasn't living on the street or in my car anymore.

Once I was settled in my new apartment, I started

reading every book I could get my hands on about software development. I taught myself data modeling, relational data base theory and systems architecture. I went on to create a program similar to Quickbooks. I actually created my program before Quickbooks, but because of my partner's greed and ego, we weren't able to succeed. I was able to sell a few on my own and made a living off of that a little while. But a few months later I was evicted from my tiny, roach-infested, basement apartment.

Because I had basically taught myself software development, my family could see that I was genuinely trying to better my position in life. They pulled together and helped me move into another apartment down the street. It was from there that I was able to get a good rest, shower, and have the clean clothes I needed to look for a job. Without my self-taught skills, my family would never have helped me get that apartment. As a result, I was able to land my first job as a software developer.

Fast Forward to Today...

I have now have a great career as a systems developer and most recently, have invented an application for a Bill Gates company. Because I don't have to worry about income anymore, I recently started working on music again. I also went back to school to pursue my 1st passion: astrophysics. Whenever I get the chance, I play poker and I play in chess tournaments. These two hobbies definitely keep my mind sharp, just like people go to the gym to keep their bodies in shape.

I took a chance on something that interested me, learned it, and now I'm doing pretty well.

Inspirations and Regrets

A couple of things have inspired me along the way. One was my passion for technology; I've enjoyed it since I was a child. First it came in the form of programming beats, and then it turned into full music production. Becoming a software developer was a natural progression from all of that. It was embedded me as far back as I can remember.

The second inspiration is my competitive nature. I competed against my stepmother's perception of who I was and what she told me I was going to become. She would always tell me that I'd never amount to anything and that I'd eventually end up in jail. She tried to ingrain that in my mind, and I knew I had to prove her wrong. In the end, I succeeded in spite of her abuse.

When I graduated high school and went on to college, I chose to move in with my music friends instead of living on campus. This circle of friends didn't support my college education, and therefore my studies suffered. It was a definite setback for my career.

I feel if I had moved on campus and surrounded myself with like-minded people, I would have fully realized my first passion instead of making all of these detours. But I've since come to realize that these detours are what shaped who I am today.

Final Gift

For the longest time, my mother never had a headstone on her grave. After getting a good job doing what I love, I was finally able to do something that no one in family could afford: give my mother a proper headstone.

Jaywill's story is one of prolific strength and accomplishment. He was able to overcome great personal tragedy and reinvent himself - and still continues to do so. He took responsibility for his life and didn't let outside sources dictate his future. Instead of becoming a victim, he chose to be the victor. He has created a life that he loves and one we can truly be inspired by.

13

Artist, Writer, Entrepreneur

"Be where your feet are..."
~ Marie Whitman

I am a native New Yorker, transplanted to Miami, Florida. I am a poet, performance artist and arts educator. I am a creative entrepreneur finding ways to smash the "Starving Artist" paradigm. I think artists have a necessary role on our planet and much needed gifts to bring to this world. For me, the arts are a way of fostering connection: connection to self, to others, to the Divine. Along my path, I've formally studied dance, yoga and massage therapy and have been writing ever since I can remember. Poetry was a way for me to express my true self, experience the world, and make sense and meaning of everything around me. In 2007, I self-published a book of poetry entitled "Signs and Wonders," which led to me diving deeper into the power of the written word and sharing it with others. I've been able to tell the truth on the page, sometimes on the stage, and transform traumas into triumph. My own poems have freed me and fed me, and now my heart's desire is to spark that kind of empowerment in others through the arts.

As a an artist and entrepreneur, my experiences include dance performance and choreography, founding an Arts Collective and studio/performance space, owning a retail dancewear business, and teaching poetry and spoken word to "at risk" teens! In 2014, I founded a poetry outreach organization called Eat Your Poem. EYP seeks to spread love and shed light through the poetic word. I am currently organizing a program called "Poetry with a Purpose," which will take Professional Poets into Women's Shelters to offer uplifting readings and creative writing workshops. We will be working with the women in the shelter on creating their own poems and then publishing a book of their poetic stories. I also have a subscription program called 30 Days/30 Poems.

Each morning, for thirty days, subscribers receive a new, original poem, written with love by yours truly. I also do what's known as "pop-up poetry" or "poetry on-demand." I set up my 1965 vintage smith corona sterling typewriter at various venues, including farmers markets and art galleries, and type poems on demand for people.

Quiet Artist

I studied dance and musical theater as a kid and ALWAYS wrote poems. The arts have always been a huge part of my life. My childhood was filled with classes and shows in dance studios and with the drama club at school. I even choreographed the junior high version of Annie and wrote and performed an original song in the high school talent show. This always lit me up, but for some strange reason I never fully embraced the power of this creative spirit within me and that it could be my way of life. It also wasn't really nurtured or acknowledged from the outside or from my parents back then, so it always felt like my own quiet storm inside. I got a marketing and communications degree and worked in the music business from 1991 through 1998, doing everything from interning and administrative assistant work to marketing and promotion and artist development. I still danced and taught dance "on the side" and wrote poems and songs "in secret." I was always a creative artist but was kind of in the closet, so to speak.

I made some of the most special friendships and relationships while working at record labels that are now life-long. I got to be around ALOT of live music. I learned a TON about artist development and marketing and then realized that my inner artist was screaming. I needed to leave this very enjoyable, mostly special, and totally cool music business behind to go salvage my badass creative self. She had things to say and do and share and create.

Breaking Free

I finally made the decision to change in the late 90's. I was working at RCA records, and working with a lot of great people, but something was missing. I was having a great time and enjoyed what I did, but it still wasn't enough. I decided that if I was ever going to pursue what I was passionate about, I'd better get going now. I finally got up the courage to quit my job and venture on a path of creativity.

The first thing I did was make the decision to leave my "stable" and "prestigious" (and pretty cool) corporate record label job. I got back to my dance study, began writing a ton, and did everything I could to nurture my creative side. I moved to Miami and floated around as a freelance dance teacher/massage therapist/performer/dancer/poet/choreographer from about 1999 to 2007, when I self-published my poetry book. This led me towards developing a writing and spoken word program for "at-risk" first-time offender teenage girls. Finally, in 2008, I founded my arts space. My life is now filled with lots of poetry and performance gigs, and I am even producing shows in my own venue and writing songs!!! It's a mixed colorful bag, and I love it.

Inspirations and Regrets

The questions and wonders of this mysterious life inspire me. Us messy human beings inspire me. I am driven to find the magical and divine within our mundane world. All of this drives me to ask and create every single day.

I wish I had believed in the power of my creative voice

sooner. But as I write that, I also know that you're ready when you're ready. Had I taken a shorter path, I would not have met certain people and developed certain relationships/friendships, which are just vital to my heart and life.

Everyone moves at their own pace. Marie never really gave up her dreams; she just kept them behind closed doors for a while until she was ready to take a leap of faith. She chose the stability of a job, and it wasn't long before she found it wasn't true to her creative self. Marie eventually gave into her dreams; her passions and let them take her on a journey of true happiness.

www.EatYourPoem.com
www.MarieWhitman.com

14

What's your story?

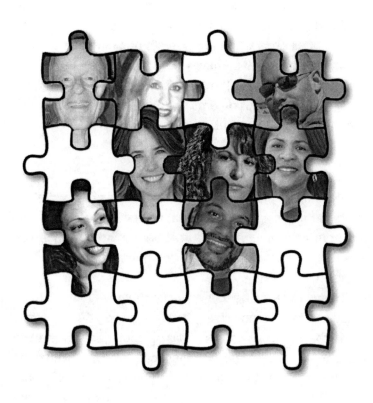

We all start out in this world exactly the same. We are all born, and we all will die. The time you have between birth and death is an incredible opportunity to create an amazing story - one you would be happy to live and would inspire others.

I hope that reading through the lives of all these people has got you thinking about your own life and the one you would love to live. You just read stories from men and women of all ages with a diverse set of circumstances and dreams. Some always knew what they wanted to do, and others found out along the way. The key is to be open to the possibilities. Let your dreams and your passions guide you into the life you truly want.

No Excuses

Remember, God gave us free will. No one can make you say or do anything you don't want to do. No one can stop you from achieving what you set your mind to. Once you take responsibility for your life, you might surprise yourself in a wonderful way.

Things might happen in your life that may make it more difficult, but not impossible. There is a saying that adversity builds character, not adversity *kills* character. Use everything you got to be the best you, you can be. Use everything you've ever been through to push you to where you want to go. There are no excuses for not living the life you want to live, the life you dream. Remember, the only thing holding you back, is you.

If you noticed while reading the stories of these extraordinary people, most of them said they regretted not pursuing their dreams sooner. After all, the sooner you get started creating the life you love, the sooner you can live it.

But if you notice, they also knew it happened just when it should have.

I believe that everything happens for a reason, good or bad. There are things we have to go through before we can get to where we want be. All of the things we go through are building a foundation for when we get there. If we "get there" before it's time, we may not stay there and get crushed; the foundation falls, and we have to start over. That's okay, if that happens we have a chance to learn from our mistakes and try again from a stronger vantage point.

Remember that pain causes change. People normally won't make a big change until they are miserable. If you tried and failed, don't be discouraged and stop trying. Where are you now? Ask yourself, "am I really happy, or am I just comfortable being uncomfortable?"

...When I Retire

I've heard many people say this, and maybe you have too: "I'll do all the things I love to do when I retire."

Many people trick themselves into thinking that they will be happy and do all of the things they love when they retire. So, they go through the most of their life - when they are healthy and strong - sticking with a job that makes them unhappy, with a "light at the end of the tunnel" attitude. That's how they push themselves through each day. The problem with this "plan" is that the future is uncertain.

I've heard stories of people working hard their whole lives and as soon as they retire, they get sick, become incapacitated, or die. The stress of being unhappy for so long may have finally caught up with them up, and they become unable to do the things they love. Why not do what you love now while you're able to enjoy it?

Let me give you an example of what could happen:

My mom's cousin is an artist. She and her husband bought a nice piece of land in Vermont that had a 100-year-old barn built on it. I went up there with them one spring, and I heard them talk about the dreams they shared. He wanted to restore the old barn, and she was going to have an art studio inside it - all things they were going to do, "when they retired." They were about 60 at the time, so retirement wasn't far away.

However, a couple of years later, the husband changed his mind. After over 40 years of marriage, he divorced her. She was devastated and still hasn't recovered today. Her dream of moving up to Vermont and creating art in that old barn died. Sadly, she hasn't bounced back and doesn't feel very creative anymore. She will probably never live the life she dreamed of living

I'm not telling you these things to scare you, I'm telling you these things because they happen. There are some people that do retire from the jobs they tolerated for years and go on to have happy lives. Still, how can you know for certain that you will be one of those lucky ones? The truth is that you don't. Again, you need to take responsibility for your own happiness. You need to create a life you love as soon as possible. Do what you love now, and don't put it on the back-burner.

Begin with the End in Mind

Taking on a new career and pursuing your dreams is a big change in anyone's life. The thought of making that big change can sometimes be overwhelming. That's why it's a good idea to make a plan; create small, doable goals that you can do one at a time.

When I get in my car to run an errand, I think about where I need to go before I get in the car. I think about where I need to be (the end in mind), and then I figure out how to get there. What steps do I need to take to get there? I need to find my keys, start the car, drive the car, I might have to stop for gas; then I need to drive and make turns, etc. (small doable goals), until I reach my destination.

It's the same with any goal. You must first think about what that is. Sometimes that's the hardest part; *knowing what you truly want*. When you figure it out, the rest should be easy. Let's look at an example.

Let's say that my passion is painting and I wanted to create art for a living, my plan would look like this:

1. Establish my passion:
    a. My passion is to paint abstracts in watercolor.
2. The end in mind:
    a. I will sell my art in a gallery.
3. Small doable goals - the steps I need to take to get there are:
    a. I will enroll in classes to learn techniques.
        i. Check the community center or community college for night classes.
    b. I will create one art piece a month for 12 months.
        i. Set aside 3 hours every Saturday to paint.
    c. While I am taking classes and creating art, I will research how I can get my art seen.
        i. Check online or in the community paper for art shows.
        ii. Ask my teacher for recommendations.
    d. I will attend art exhibits and build relationships with other artists and gallery owners.

                i. I will attend at least art one exhibit per month.
        e. I will show my best 3 pieces to the art gallery owners I have built relationships with.
        f. The gallery owner will display my art.
4. I will sell my art in a gallery.

You see how I took each goal and broke it down into smaller goals? Each one of those smaller goals supported and helped me to achieve the larger goal. You can break them down even further if you like. The "end in mind" was the beginning of my plan, and the last thing on my goal list matched it.

So, what are you waiting for? Go for it! Be one of those extra-ordinary people who had the courage to create a life they love. And when you do, please share your story with me!

Give a Testimonial:
www.growingupforgrownups.com

Share on Facebook:
www.facebook.com/GrowingUpForGrownUps

Follow us on Twitter: @growupgrownup

More information and templates for goal planning can be found by visiting www.growingupforgrownups.com.

15

Reflection

Sometimes I'll hear or read something that causes me to think more deeply about myself and/or whatever I'm going through at the time. Sometimes it lights a fire under me or pushes me to move forward on something - whether it be my own personal growth or a project I'm working on.

If the real stories from these real people have lit a little glow, it is my hope that one of these carefully selected quotes will fan a flame, and help give you the courage you need to create a life you love.

My favorite comes from a movie - don't laugh! It's perfect:

"If you only do what you can do,
you will never be more than you are now."
~ Po, character in "Kung Fu Panda 3"

"The secret of getting ahead is getting started."
~ Samuel L. Clemens aka Mark Twain, American Author and Humorist

"If you do not change direction,
you may end up where you are heading."
~ Lao Tzu, Ancient Chinese Philosopher and Writer

"The future belongs to those who believe
in the beauty of their dreams."
~ Eleanor Roosevelt, American Politician, Diplomat, and Activist

"Life isn't about finding yourself. Life is about creating yourself."
 ~ George Bernard Shaw, Irish Playwright, Critic and Controversialist

"You are never too old to reinvent yourself."
 ~ Steve Harvey, American Entertainer

"Your life does not get better by chance, it gets better by change."
 ~ Jim Rohn, American Entrepreneur, Author and Motivational Speaker

"If you want something you've never had, you must be willing to do something you've never done."
 ~ Unknown

"You only live once, but if you do it right, once is enough."
 ~ Mae West, American Entertainer

Or another way to look at it:

"It isn't true that you live only once. You only die once. You live lots of times, if you know how."
 ~ Bobby Darin, American Entertainer

"Do you want to know who you are? Don't ask. Act! Action will delineate and define you."
 ~ Thomas Jefferson, American Founding Father

"It takes courage to grow up and become who you really are."
 ~ E. E. Cummings, American Poet, Painter, Essayist, Author, and Playwright

"We only regret the chances we didn't take, the relationships we were afraid to have, and the decisions we waited too long to make."
~ Lewis Carroll, English Writer, Mathematician, Logician, Anglican Deacon, and Photographer

CPSIA information can be obtained
at www.ICGtesting.com
Printed in the USA
FSOW02n0814250916
25363FS